Concept and Development
Miguel Kagan

Designer: Alex Core
Illustrator: Erin Kant
Copyeditor: Ginny Harvey
Publications Manager: Becky Herrington

Kagan

Kagan Publishing
981 Calle Amanecer
San Clemente, CA 92673
1 (800) 933-2667
www.KaganOnline.com

ISBN: 978-1-933445-27-4

Classbuilding Questions
TABLE OF CONTENTS

Question Card Sets

Classbuilding Questions
INTRODUCTION

QUICK OVERVIEW

This book offers a super simple, yet incredibly effective, way to do classbuilding. If you haven't noticed already, the book is brimming with question cards. There are 20 sets of questions and 20 question cards for each set. If my math is correct, that's 400 question cards in all! The question sets are all based on topics students love to talk about. We developed question sets on a variety of fun-to-discuss topics, including Birthdays Favorites, Sports, Television, and more.

To play, each student receives a question card. Using Mix-Pair-Share or Travel-N-Tell (two classbuilding structures described in detail on the following pages), students pair up to ask classmates the question on their card and to respond to classmates' questions. The stimulating questions and engaging process build classroom bonds. Classmates get to know, like, and respect each other more. Students interact with classmates in a fun and friendly way. It makes the classroom a safe place to learn and creates a more cooperative and caring classroom climate.

If you're ready to get started, feel free to skip ahead to the Structures section. While you can use the questions in this book without using structures, you and your students will get more out of the process by using the simple classbuilding structures provided. If you're new to classbuilding or want to explore this concept in a little more depth, read on!

WHAT IS CLASSBUILDING?

Generally speaking, classbuilding refers to activities designed to enrich the class climate and make the classroom a kinder, safer place to learn. The goals of classbuilding are for students to get acquainted, for the class to forge an identity, for students to feel mutually supported by classmates, to understand and respect individual differences, and to develop synergy on the contributions of classmates.

A key element to classbuilding is students interact with each other. When using cooperative teams, it is important that students interact with classmates outside of their teams. With teams, students often build strong bonds with teammates, especially with regular teambuilding. Classbuilding encourages students to interact with many different classmates. That almost always means students are up and out of their seats, interacting with their classmates. Students enjoy the action, which contributes to positive class tone. Students sense the classroom is a place where they get to get up and do stuff. "*We don't just sit quietly in our seats all day long!*"

Classbuilding is usually a brief break from academic work. The class takes a little time off academics to focus on fun and relationship building. Classbuilding does require a little time off the curriculum and a little effort on the part of the teacher to create worthwhile activities. Is the investment worth it? Absolutely! And with this book, we hope to minimize the effort you have to exert to reap the benefits of classbuilding.

WHY IS CLASSBUILDING IMPORTANT?

One good question deserves another. Ask yourself, *"Why do we send kids to school?"* To learn? To equip them with the skills they'll need to succeed in life? Right and right! Classbuilding helps us reach both of these objectives. Take learning. Could it be true that students actually learn more by taking some time off academics to build interpersonal relationships? To have a little fun? The answer is a resounding, "Yes!"

Educators are becoming more aware of the power of the context of learning and the impact it has on students' ability to learn. We can probably thank brain science for these insights or at least for the widespread acceptance of what good teachers *already* knew. Different brain-based learning theorists have different sets of principles that they espouse. However, there seems to be almost universal acceptance of this basic premise: Learning is inhibited by threat. Are there threats within your classroom? From your perspective, maybe not. But take the perspective of some of your students. They fear social evaluation. Students are often

afraid that they're just not as smart as some of their fellow classmates. There is the fear of social ostracism. Students fear they are different and that they just don't fit in. And we know all too well, the very real physical threat of bullying exists. Unfortunately, bullying runs rampant in schools, from subtle intimidation to outright violence. There is also the fear of failure.

For children developing their own sense of identity, school can indeed be a scary place. And it is these perceived threats that interfere with students' ability to concentrate and learn. Classbuilding is important because the activities are perhaps the best remedies we have for eradicating those threats and removing barriers to meaningful learning. With classbuilding, we reorient students with activities that are fun. Students get to know and like others who they may otherwise have no interactions with. As they interact, that stranger is no longer a stranger but more of a friend. Classbuilding turns the classroom into a safer, more caring place for students to learn. Students are freer to take risks in an environment where they feel accepted and supported than in an environment where they are apprehensive. Free from perceived thoughts in the classroom, their minds are free to focus on learning.

Another principle of brain-based learning is this: physiology affects learning. This includes internal states and moods. Students who like class, the teacher, and fellow classmates are happier and more optimistic. They have a more positive outlook on school and learning. And learning improves. Classbuilding has a positive impact on students' physiology. It puts students in a happy, optimistic frame of mind, ideal for learning.

Belonging is hugely important to students. Students are less likely to drop out when they feel they belong and that others care about them as people and want to see them succeed. Classbuilding combats apathy, bullying, and drop out. It puts students on the same side.

In addition to creating a safer, more caring learning environment, classbuilding prepares students for the real world with personal and social skills. Through these activities, students will interact with all their classmates. They will share information about themselves and hear information about others that is often quite different. It will expose students to new ways of thinking about things. It will open their eyes to different perspectives on the world. It'll broaden their minds.

Prejudice and racism stems from a lack of understanding and respect for others who are different. Classbuilding offers students the opportunity to transcend superficial barriers and get to know and celebrate classmates as unique individuals.

Students who leave school with diversity skills are more prepared for the world of tomorrow than those who work independently and maintain a narrow view of the world and each other.

WHAT'S IN THIS BOOK?

In this book, you will find a treasure trove of classbuilding questions to be used with two terrific classbuilding structures.

Classbuilding Questions

The book contains 400 ready-to-use question cards. The cards are organized into 20 discussion topics with 20 question cards per set. You can do a terrific, quick classbuilding activity in a few minutes with just one or two questions. With hundreds of cards, you'll have enough content here for hours and hours of classbuilding activities. While you'll probably want to mix it up and do other types of classbuilding activities during the school year, this book will provide a seemingly endless supply of questions. So if you want a quick classbuilding activity, but don't want to do any prep, pull out a question or a question card set and use these go-to staples.

The topics were selected based on things students like to discuss. The questions encourage students to share things about themselves, what they like, what they dislike, their opinions on issues. The questions promote discussion. They promote interaction. And they create fun!

Classbuilding Structures

Structures are cooperative instructional strategies. You could use the classbuilding questions in this book as whole-class questions. But good classbuilding leverages the basic principles of cooperative learning. We use the acronym PIES to symbolize the four principles we take as core to cooperative learning. Here's how the principles relate to classbuilding:

Positive Interdependence
The task is structured so that students work together. They feel like they are on the same side.

Individual Accountability
Each student is accountable for doing something, so no student can hide.

Equal Participation
Students participate about equally.

Simultaneous Interaction
Interaction is going on in each pair. If you took a snapshot of the classroom, it would show a high degree of active engagement going on within each pair.

In this book, we feature two structures we encourage you to use with your students: Mix-Pair-Share and Travel-N-Tell. In Mix-Pair-Share, students "mix" about the room, "pair" up with a classmate, then take turns "sharing" the response to each other's questions. In Travel-N-Tell, the class is divided in half. Half are A's and the other half B's. A's and B's alternate to "travel" to find a new partner, then "tell" their partner their response.

WHEN SHOULD I USE THESE ACTIVITIES?

- **Weekly**—Taking a little time off academics once a week to do a little classbuilding is worth it. You can schedule the time of the week. For example, Friday Classbuilding for 10 minutes. Alternatively, for a little novelty, you can spring a fun classbuilding activity on the class.

- **Conflicts and Tension**—Classbuilding is a great way to boost class morale. If things are tense, you become aware of bullying, or students are having conflicts, classbuilding can quickly transform the classroom environment into a more fun and friendly place to be.

- **New Students**—If you have a new student in the class, it's a good idea to do a little classbuilding. It's only natural for students to want to get to know the new classmate. It's better to provide a structured forum for getting acquainted than for students' natural inquisitiveness to interfere with what you're trying to teach.

- **Stress Reliever**—Do you or your students ever feel stressed out? How about before or after testing? Classbuilders are fun to do and you'll see the tension literally leave their bodies as they engage in fun-to-discuss questions. And, for you too!

- **Brain-Breaks**–Break up a long block of mathematics with a quick classbuilder. Use the classbuilders as state changers. The classbuilders involve discussion and interaction so they work as a great state changer anytime students are doing other types of tasks such as writing, solving problems, reading, etc.

- **Energizers**–If you notice the energy level in the class is getting low, reach for a classbuilder. Students get to talk about things they like. Without fail, classbuilding questions raise the class energy level.

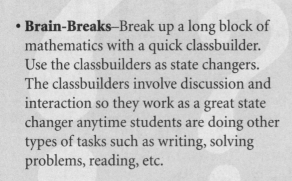

Question Card Tips

Each question is provided on its own question card. Individual question cards make the activity more game-like and help focus students on one question at a time. Here are a few tips for your classbuilding question cards:

- **Class Sets**—Copy two sets of cards on each topic so you have enough question cards for each student. There are 20 cards per set, so if you have 32 students, there will be 12 students who have a duplicate card. This is fine because students pair with new partners each time so the chance of the same two students getting the same question is extremely low.

- **Colored Paper**—Copy different sets onto different color paper to make them more colorful and easier to see at a glance that they are different sets.

- **Card Stock**—Copy the questions onto card-stock paper so the cards are more durable.

- **Laminate Cards**—Laminate the cards for extra durability.

- **Storing Cards**—Wrap a rubber band around each set of cards to keep the set together. That makes it really easy to give each team their own set of cards. Or, keep sets together with an alligator clip or inside an envelope.

MIX-PAIR-SHARE

The class "mixes" until the teacher calls "pair." Students pair up to respond to each other's question card for the allotted time.

▶ **GETTING READY:**

- Each student receives a question card.

- The teacher prepares music to play while students mix (optional).

Pair

2 Teacher Calls "Pair"

After a few seconds of mixing around the room, the teacher stops the music and tells students to pair up.

1 Students Mix

Students mix around the room trading question cards with classmates they pass. To make the mixing more interesting, play some music as students mix.

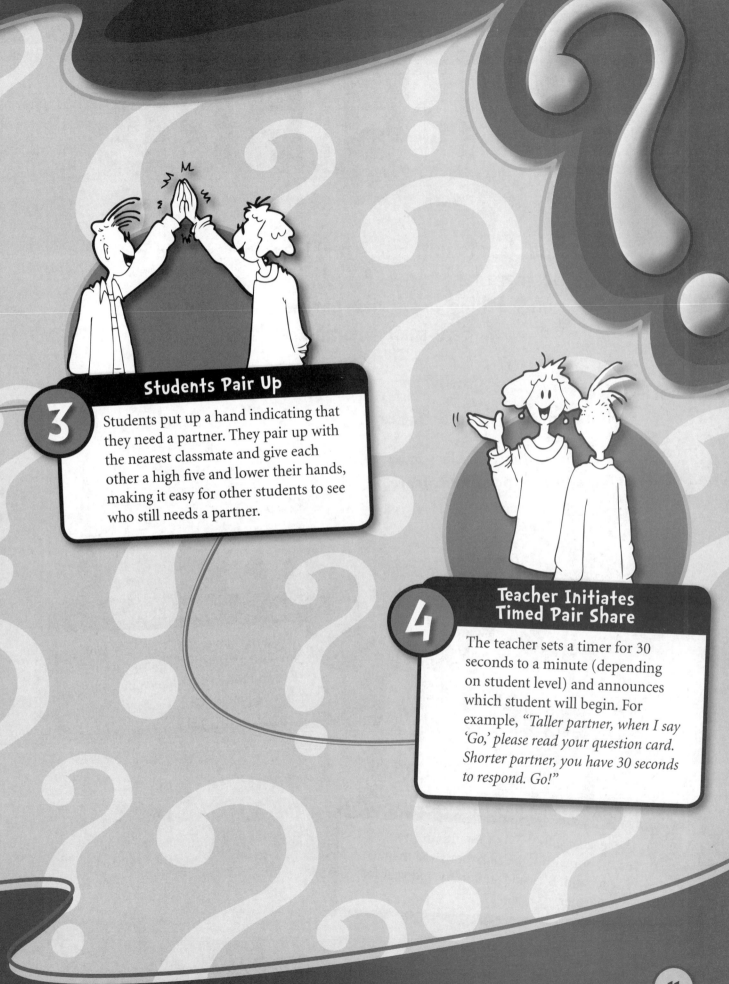

Students Pair Up

3

Students put up a hand indicating that they need a partner. They pair up with the nearest classmate and give each other a high five and lower their hands, making it easy for other students to see who still needs a partner.

Teacher Initiates Timed Pair Share

4

The teacher sets a timer for 30 seconds to a minute (depending on student level) and announces which student will begin. For example, *"Taller partner, when I say 'Go,' please read your question card. Shorter partner, you have 30 seconds to respond. Go!"*

TRAVEL-N-TELL

The class is split into A and B partners. A and B partners take turns "traveling" to new partners and "telling" their new partners their answer to their question cards.

▶ **GETTING READY:**

- Each student receives a question card.

- The teacher divides the class in half. Half are A's and the other half are B's.

2 A's Travel

A's raise a hand and "travel" to pair up with a B partner. They give a high five and lower their hands indicating they've paired up.

1 B's Stand and Spread Out

The teacher tells the B's to stand up and spread out within the classroom and then to raise a hand. B's stand stationary and wait for an A partner.

Classbuilding Questions
Kagan Publishing • (800) 933-2667 • www.KaganOnline.com

A's Tell

3 B's read A's their question card and A's "tell" B's their answer.

B's Respond

4 B's appreciate A's for sharing by giving a verbal response and/or a physical response (see Sample Responses and Celebrations on page 15).

(CONTINUED...)

B's Travel

5 A's and B's raise their hands again. Now A's stand stationary and B's "travel" to pair up with a new A partner. They give a high five and lower their hands indicating they've paired up.

My favorite...

B's Tell

6 A's read B's their question card and B's "tell" A's their answer.

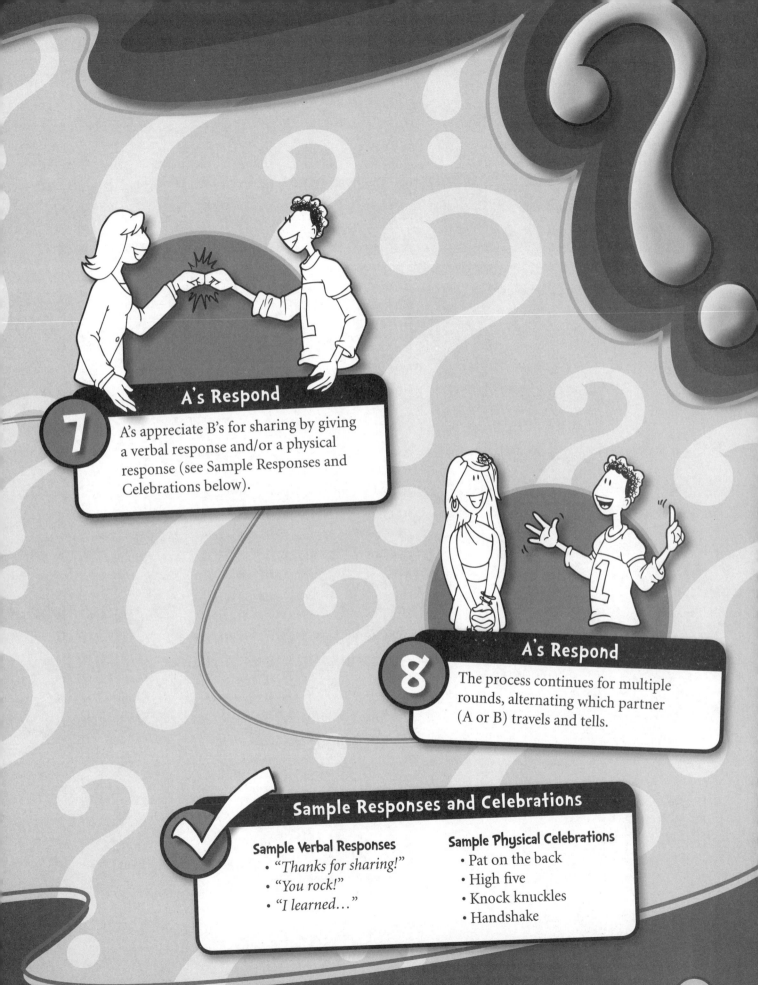

7 A's Respond

A's appreciate B's for sharing by giving a verbal response and/or a physical response (see Sample Responses and Celebrations below).

8 A's Respond

The process continues for multiple rounds, alternating which partner (A or B) travels and tells.

Sample Responses and Celebrations

Sample Verbal Responses
- *"Thanks for sharing!"*
- *"You rock!"*
- *"I learned…"*

Sample Physical Celebrations
- Pat on the back
- High five
- Knock knuckles
- Handshake

card set
#**1**

AGREE OR DISAGREE?

AGREE OR DISAGREE?
Question Cards

① AGREE OR DISAGREE?

Human cloning should be legal. Do you agree or disagree? Explain your stance.

② AGREE OR DISAGREE?

Flag burning should be illegal. Do you agree or disagree? Explain your stance.

③ AGREE OR DISAGREE?

Animal testing should be legal. Do you agree or disagree? Explain your stance.

④ AGREE OR DISAGREE?

Nuclear power plants are too dangerous. Do you agree or disagree? Explain your stance.

AGREE OR DISAGREE?
Question Cards

⑤ AGREE OR DISAGREE?

Torture should be illegal, even in wartime. Do you agree or disagree? Explain your stance.

Classbuilding Questions • © Kagan Publishing

⑥ AGREE OR DISAGREE?

Wearing a helmet or seatbelt should be a personal choice not a law. Do you agree or disagree? Explain your stance.

Classbuilding Questions • © Kagan Publishing

⑦ AGREE OR DISAGREE?

People should be required to serve in the military for one year after high school. Do you agree or disagree? Explain your stance.

Classbuilding Questions • © Kagan Publishing

⑧ AGREE OR DISAGREE?

Drugs and alcohol are harmful and should be made illegal. Do you agree or disagree? Explain your stance.

Classbuilding Questions • © Kagan Publishing

AGREE OR DISAGREE?
Question Cards

⑨ AGREE OR DISAGREE?

People who are caught polluting should have to spend a night in jail. Do you agree or disagree? Explain your stance.

Classbuilding Questions • © Kagan Publishing

⑩ AGREE OR DISAGREE?

Guns are dangerous and should be completely outlawed. Do you agree or disagree? Explain your stance.

Classbuilding Questions • © Kagan Publishing

⑪ AGREE OR DISAGREE?

If someone is very ill, it should be their choice whether they want to live or die. Do you agree or disagree? Explain your stance.

Classbuilding Questions • © Kagan Publishing

⑫ AGREE OR DISAGREE?

People should be allowed to live in any country they want. Do you agree or disagree? Explain your stance.

Classbuilding Questions • © Kagan Publishing

AGREE OR DISAGREE?
Question Cards

---

13 AGREE OR DISAGREE?

The government should be allowed to sentence people to death. Do you agree or disagree? Explain your stance.

Classbuilding Questions • © Kagan Publishing

---

14 AGREE OR DISAGREE?

Violent sports such as boxing should be outlawed. Do you agree or disagree? Explain your stance.

Classbuilding Questions • © Kagan Publishing

---

15 AGREE OR DISAGREE?

Children should be allowed to vote for the President. Do you agree or disagree? Explain your stance.

Classbuilding Questions • © Kagan Publishing

---

16 AGREE OR DISAGREE?

The principal should have the right to decide a student's punishment, including swatting. Do you agree or disagree? Explain your stance.

Classbuilding Questions • © Kagan Publishing

AGREE OR DISAGREE?
Question Cards

(17) AGREE OR DISAGREE?

Downloading music on the Internet is the same as stealing a CD from a store. Do you agree or disagree? Explain your stance.

Classbuilding Questions • © Kagan Publishing

(18) AGREE OR DISAGREE?

Talking or texting on the phone while driving should be legal. Do you agree or disagree? Explain your stance.

Classbuilding Questions • © Kagan Publishing

(19) AGREE OR DISAGREE?

For safety, everyone should have to carry an ID card and show it to an official if asked. Do you agree or disagree? Explain your stance.

Classbuilding Questions • © Kagan Publishing

(20) AGREE OR DISAGREE?

Every person should be required to pass a parenting class before being allowed to have children. Do you agree or disagree? Explain your stance.

Classbuilding Questions • © Kagan Publishing

Classbuilding Questions
Kagan Publishing • (800) 933-2667 • www.KaganOnline.com

AGREE OR DISAGREE?
Journal Writing Question

Torture should be illegal, even in wartime. Do you agree or disagree? Explain your stance.

_____

_____

_____

_____

_____

_____

_____

_____

_____

_____

_____

_____

_____

_____

_____

_____

AGREE OR DISAGREE?
Journal Writing Question

Talking or texting on the phone while driving should be legal. Do you agree or disagree? Explain your stance.

_____

_____

_____

_____

_____

_____

_____

_____

_____

_____

_____

_____

_____

_____

_____

_____

_____

Classbuilding Questions
Kagan Publishing • (800) 933-2667 • www.KaganOnline.com

card set
#**2**

BIRTHDAYS

BIRTHDAYS
Question Cards

---

① BIRTHDAYS

What is the best birthday present you've ever received? What did you like about it?

Classbuilding Questions • © Kagan Publishing

---

② BIRTHDAYS

What is the best birthday present you've ever given? Why was it such a great gift?

Classbuilding Questions • © Kagan Publishing

---

③ BIRTHDAYS

Do you like the time of year when you were born? Why or why not?

Classbuilding Questions • © Kagan Publishing

---

④ BIRTHDAYS

If you could plan the perfect birthday party for yourself, what would it be?

Classbuilding Questions • © Kagan Publishing

Classbuilding Questions
Kagan Publishing • (800) 933-2667 • www.KaganOnline.com

BIRTHDAYS
Question Cards

---

5   **BIRTHDAYS**

What is the most fun birthday party you've ever had? Describe.

Classbuilding Questions • © Kagan Publishing

---

6   **BIRTHDAYS**

If you could receive any gift for your next birthday, what would it be? Why would you ask for that gift?

Classbuilding Questions • © Kagan Publishing

---

7   **BIRTHDAYS**

What do you typically do at your birthday party? Describe.

Classbuilding Questions • © Kagan Publishing

---

8   **BIRTHDAYS**

What friend's birthday party is the best you've ever been to? Describe it.

Classbuilding Questions • © Kagan Publishing

BIRTHDAYS
Question Cards

⑨ BIRTHDAYS

If you could have one birthday wish come true, what would you wish for? Why?

Classbuilding Questions • © Kagan Publishing

⑩ BIRTHDAYS

Have you ever had a surprise party? If so, how did you like it? If not, would you want a surprise party? Why or why not?

Classbuilding Questions • © Kagan Publishing

⑪ BIRTHDAYS

Do you do anything special for your birthday with your family? Describe.

Classbuilding Questions • © Kagan Publishing

⑫ BIRTHDAYS

What is your best birthday memory? Describe it.

Classbuilding Questions • © Kagan Publishing

Classbuilding Questions
Kagan Publishing • (800) 933-2667 • www.KaganOnline.com

BIRTHDAYS
Question Cards

---

13 **BIRTHDAYS**

What is your favorite birthday game or activity? Describe it.

Classbuilding Questions • © Kagan Publishing

---

14 **BIRTHDAYS**

If you could stay one age for the rest of your life, what age would you choose? Why?

Classbuilding Questions • © Kagan Publishing

---

15 **BIRTHDAYS**

Does it make you happy when people make a big deal about your birthday? Why or why not? Why do you think people make a big deal?

Classbuilding Questions • © Kagan Publishing

---

16 **BIRTHDAYS**

What is the nicest thing someone has ever done for you on your birthday? Explain.

Classbuilding Questions • © Kagan Publishing

BIRTHDAYS
Question Cards

---

⑰ BIRTHDAYS

What do you look forward to about getting older? Explain.

Classbuilding Questions • © Kagan Publishing

---

⑱ BIRTHDAYS

Birthdays are awesome! Do you agree or disagree? Why do you feel this way?

Classbuilding Questions • © Kagan Publishing

---

⑲ BIRTHDAYS

Would you rather have a big birthday party with lots of friends or a small party with a few close friends?

Classbuilding Questions • © Kagan Publishing

---

⑳ BIRTHDAYS

If your best friend was having a birthday, what would you write in his or her birthday card?

Classbuilding Questions • © Kagan Publishing

Classbuilding Questions
Kagan Publishing • (800) 933-2667 • www.KaganOnline.com

BIRTHDAYS
Journal Writing Question

What is the best birthday present you've ever given? Why was it such a great gift?

BIRTHDAYS
Journal Writing Question

If you could stay one age for the rest of your life, what age would you choose? Why?

_____

_____

_____

_____

_____

_____

_____

_____

_____

_____

_____

_____

_____

_____

_____

_____

_____

_____

Classbuilding Questions
Kagan Publishing • (800) 933-2667 • www.KaganOnline.com

card set
3

BULLYING

BULLYING
Question Cards

---

① BULLYING

What are some things you could do if someone was bullying you? Explain.

Classbuilding Questions • © Kagan Publishing

---

② BULLYING

What would you do if you saw your best friend being bullied? Explain.

Classbuilding Questions • © Kagan Publishing

---

③ BULLYING

Why do you think some kids bully other kids?

Classbuilding Questions • © Kagan Publishing

---

④ BULLYING

Have you ever been a bully? If so, in what way? How do you feel about it? If not, explain why not.

Classbuilding Questions • © Kagan Publishing

Classbuilding Questions
Kagan Publishing • (800) 933-2667 • www.KaganOnline.com

BULLYING
Question Cards

5 **BULLYING**

What could you do to help a student feel better who had been bullied?

Classbuilding Questions • © Kagan Publishing

6 **BULLYING**

Do you think there is anything you can do or say so that you are not bullied? Explain.

Classbuilding Questions • © Kagan Publishing

7 **BULLYING**

Do you think bullies pick on a certain type of kid or are they bullies to everyone? Explain.

Classbuilding Questions • © Kagan Publishing

8 **BULLYING**

How could you tell on a bully without fearing that the bully might come after you?

Classbuilding Questions • © Kagan Publishing

BULLYING
Question Cards

---

⑨ BULLYING

If you told on a bully and other kids called you a tattletale or snitch, what would you do? Describe how you think they might feel about you after that.

---

⑩ BULLYING

What's worse: Being hit, being called names, or being bossed around? Explain what you think is the worst type of treatment and why.

---

⑪ BULLYING

Is excluding someone from the group the same as bullying? Explain your answer.

---

⑫ BULLYING

Have you ever felt pressure by someone else to tease or treat another person mean? Explain.

BULLYING
Question Cards

13 BULLYING

If kids are bullied, should they always report it to an adult? Explain your position.

Classbuilding Questions • © Kagan Publishing

14 BULLYING

Have you ever helped a person in need? If yes, what did you do? If no, would you help? Why or why not?

Classbuilding Questions • © Kagan Publishing

15 BULLYING

Are bullies bad people or good people with bad behaviors? Explain.

Classbuilding Questions • © Kagan Publishing

16 BULLYING

Who could you turn to if you were being bullied? What would you say?

Classbuilding Questions • © Kagan Publishing

BULLYING
Question Cards

17 **BULLYING**

What would be a fair punishment for a bully? Explain.

Classbuilding Questions • © Kagan Publishing

18 **BULLYING**

What are some things you could do to make your school bully-free?

Classbuilding Questions • © Kagan Publishing

19 **BULLYING**

What's worse: Aggressive behaviors or aggressive words? Describe your opinion.

Classbuilding Questions • © Kagan Publishing

20 **BULLYING**

Is bullying different between boys and girls? Describe your opinion.

Classbuilding Questions • © Kagan Publishing

Classbuilding Questions
Kagan Publishing • (800) 933-2667 • www.KaganOnline.com

BULLYING
Journal Writing Question

What could you do to help a student feel better who had been bullied?

BULLYING
Journal Writing Question

Have you ever helped a person in need? If yes, what did you do? If no, would you help? Why or why not?

Classbuilding Questions
Kagan Publishing • (800) 933-2667 • www.KaganOnline.com

card set
#4

CHARACTER

CHARACTER
Question Cards

CHARACTER

1

What does being loyal mean to you? Who or what are you loyal to and why?

Classbuilding Questions • © Kagan Publishing

CHARACTER

2

Who is the most patient person you know? Is it good or bad to be that patient? Explain.

Classbuilding Questions • © Kagan Publishing

CHARACTER

3

Have you ever felt like quitting? Describe the situation and what you did.

Classbuilding Questions • © Kagan Publishing

CHARACTER

4

What are your responsibilities? How would you rate yourself on meeting your responsibilities?

Classbuilding Questions • © Kagan Publishing

Classbuilding Questions
Kagan Publishing • (800) 933-2667 • www.KaganOnline.com

CHARACTER
Question Cards

CHARACTER

⑤

Is there ever a time when it is okay not to be honest? Describe.

Classbuilding Questions • © Kagan Publishing

CHARACTER

⑥

How is being courageous different from being fearless? Describe a time when you were courageous.

Classbuilding Questions • © Kagan Publishing

CHARACTER

⑦

Describe a time when you knew you were doing the wrong thing, but did it anyway. How did you feel about it? What was the result?

Classbuilding Questions • © Kagan Publishing

CHARACTER

⑧

Does everyone deserve the same amount of respect or do some people deserve more or less? Explain your position.

Classbuilding Questions • © Kagan Publishing

CHARACTER
Question Cards

CHARACTER

9

What are some things you can do and say to show you care for someone?

CHARACTER

10

What is a big mistake you've made? How did you handle it?

CHARACTER

11

Would you consider yourself to be a hard worker? Why or why not? Do others consider you to be a hard worker? Why or why not?

CHARACTER

12

Who is your hero? What traits or qualities does he or she have that you admire most?

Classbuilding Questions
Kagan Publishing • (800) 933-2667 • www.KaganOnline.com

CHARACTER
Question Cards

CHARACTER

(13) How would you define the word "character"?

CHARACTER

(14) What character traits do you value the most? How can you develop these traits?

CHARACTER

(15) Describe a book you've read that has a message about the importance of character.

CHARACTER

(16) Would you stand for what's right even if that meant you'd stand alone? Describe.

CHARACTER
Question Cards

CHARACTER

(17) Do you act the same when no one is watching as you do when someone is watching? Describe.

Classbuilding Questions • © Kagan Publishing

CHARACTER

(18) How do your friends reflect your character? Explain.

Classbuilding Questions • © Kagan Publishing

CHARACTER

(19) What are the advantages of living a life of positive character?

Classbuilding Questions • © Kagan Publishing

CHARACTER

(20) What is one thing about your character that you'd like to improve and why?

Classbuilding Questions • © Kagan Publishing

Classbuilding Questions
Kagan Publishing • (800) 933-2667 • www.KaganOnline.com

CHARACTER
Journal Writing Question

What are your responsibilities? How would you rate yourself on meeting your responsibilities?

_____

_____

_____

_____

_____

_____

_____

_____

_____

_____

_____

_____

_____

_____

_____

_____

_____

Who is your hero? What traits or qualities does he or she have that you admire most?

_____

_____

_____

_____

_____

_____

_____

_____

_____

_____

_____

_____

_____

_____

_____

_____

Classbuilding Questions
Kagan Publishing • (800) 933-2667 • www.KaganOnline.com

card set
#**5**

FAVORITES

FAVORITES
Question Cards

① FAVORITES

What is the best book you've ever read? Describe it.

② FAVORITES

What is your favorite season? Why? What can you do during this season that you cannot do during others?

③ FAVORITES

Who is your favorite actor? In what movie do you like him or her best?

④ FAVORITES

Who is your favorite singer or band? What song do you like best and why?

Classbuilding Questions
Kagan Publishing • (800) 933-2667 • www.KaganOnline.com

FAVORITES
Question Cards

5 **FAVORITES**

If you could only have your favorite food for dinner every night, what would you choose? Why?

Classbuilding Questions • © Kagan Publishing

6 **FAVORITES**

What is your favorite game to play? Describe it to someone who's never played it before.

Classbuilding Questions • © Kagan Publishing

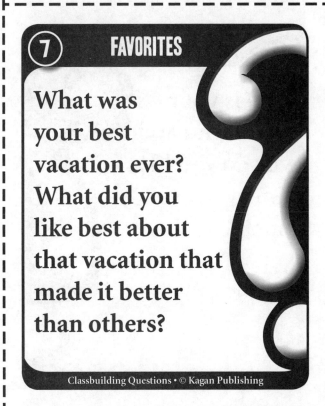

7 **FAVORITES**

What was your best vacation ever? What did you like best about that vacation that made it better than others?

Classbuilding Questions • © Kagan Publishing

8 **FAVORITES**

What or who is your favorite sports team or athlete? Why?

Classbuilding Questions • © Kagan Publishing

FAVORITES
Question Cards

9 FAVORITES

What is the best dessert ever? Describe it and the last time you ate it.

Classbuilding Questions • © Kagan Publishing

10 FAVORITES

What is the best gift you've ever received? Why did you like it so much?

Classbuilding Questions • © Kagan Publishing

11 FAVORITES

What was your favorite birthday party that you had? What did you do at the birthday party?

Classbuilding Questions • © Kagan Publishing

12 FAVORITES

Who is your best friend and why do you like him or her so much?

Classbuilding Questions • © Kagan Publishing

Classbuilding Questions
Kagan Publishing • (800) 933-2667 • www.KaganOnline.com

FAVORITES
Question Cards

13 FAVORITES

If you could wear only one color for the rest of your life what color would you choose and why?

Classbuilding Questions • © Kagan Publishing

14 FAVORITES

What is the best movie you've ever seen? Describe it to somebody who's never seen it before.

Classbuilding Questions • © Kagan Publishing

15 FAVORITES

What is your favorite month of the year? Why do you like that month better than other months of the year?

Classbuilding Questions • © Kagan Publishing

16 FAVORITES

What is your favorite store? Why do you like it so much?

Classbuilding Questions • © Kagan Publishing

FAVORITES
Question Cards

17 FAVORITES

What is your favorite holiday of the year? What do you do during the holiday that you enjoy so much?

Classbuilding Questions • © Kagan Publishing

18 FAVORITES

What is your favorite fast food restaurant? Why? What do you order when you eat there?

Classbuilding Questions • © Kagan Publishing

19 FAVORITES

What is your favorite subject in school? Why is it your favorite? Tell something interesting about it that others may not know.

Classbuilding Questions • © Kagan Publishing

20 FAVORITES

What is your favorite article of clothing? Why do you like it so much and when do you wear it?

Classbuilding Questions • © Kagan Publishing

Classbuilding Questions
Kagan Publishing • (800) 933-2667 • www.KaganOnline.com

FAVORITES
Journal Writing Question

What is your favorite season? Why? What can you do during this season that you cannot do during others?

_____

_____

_____

_____

_____

_____

_____

_____

_____

_____

_____

_____

_____

_____

_____

_____

_____

_____

_____

FAVORITES
Journal Writing Question

What is your favorite subject in school? Why is it your favorite? Tell something interesting about it that others may not know.

_____

_____

_____

_____

_____

_____

_____

_____

_____

_____

_____

_____

_____

_____

_____

_____

_____

_____

_____

_____

Classbuilding Questions
Kagan Publishing • (800) 933-2667 • www.KaganOnline.com

card set
#6

GETTING TO KNOW YOU

GETTING TO KNOW YOU
Question Cards

---

1 | **GETTING TO KNOW YOU**

Do you have any superstitions? If yes, what are they? If no, what superstitions have you seen in others?

Classbuilding Questions • © Kagan Publishing

---

2 | **GETTING TO KNOW YOU**

Do you believe that everything happens for a reason or things just randomly happen? Explain.

Classbuilding Questions • © Kagan Publishing

---

3 | **GETTING TO KNOW YOU**

What are the three coolest things you own? Describe them.

Classbuilding Questions • © Kagan Publishing

---

4 | **GETTING TO KNOW YOU**

Describe your dream house. Where is it? What does it look like?

Classbuilding Questions • © Kagan Publishing

GETTING TO KNOW YOU
Question Cards

5 | **GETTING TO KNOW YOU**

Describe how your room is decorated and what it says about you.

Classbuilding Questions • © Kagan Publishing

6 | **GETTING TO KNOW YOU**

What scares you? Tell about something that frightened you.

Classbuilding Questions • © Kagan Publishing

7 | **GETTING TO KNOW YOU**

What are three positive qualities about you? Describe them in detail.

Classbuilding Questions • © Kagan Publishing

8 | **GETTING TO KNOW YOU**

What was the most daring thing you've ever done? What were the circumstances?

Classbuilding Questions • © Kagan Publishing

GETTING TO KNOW YOU
Question Cards

⑨ GETTING TO KNOW YOU

When you spend money, what do you usually buy? Why? Explain a typical shopping trip for this item.

Classbuilding Questions • © Kagan Publishing

⑩ GETTING TO KNOW YOU

What is something that you wish more people knew about you? How would that help them know you better?

Classbuilding Questions • © Kagan Publishing

⑪ GETTING TO KNOW YOU

What is the worst injury or accident you've ever had? Explain how it happened.

Classbuilding Questions • © Kagan Publishing

⑫ GETTING TO KNOW YOU

What is your favorite kind of art? Who is your favorite artist? Why?

Classbuilding Questions • © Kagan Publishing

Classbuilding Questions
Kagan Publishing • (800) 933-2667 • www.KaganOnline.com

GETTING TO KNOW YOU
Question Cards

---

13 GETTING TO KNOW YOU

How have you changed recently? Why do you think you are changing?

Classbuilding Questions • © Kagan Publishing

---

14 GETTING TO KNOW YOU

Do you think it is better to donate money to charity or give your time and talents to others? Why?

Classbuilding Questions • © Kagan Publishing

---

15 GETTING TO KNOW YOU

How would you describe your sense of style or fashion? How do you like to dress?

Classbuilding Questions • © Kagan Publishing

---

16 GETTING TO KNOW YOU

If you could be in the Olympics, what sport would you want to compete in and why?

Classbuilding Questions • © Kagan Publishing

GETTING TO KNOW YOU
Question Cards

17 | **GETTING TO KNOW YOU**

What was the last nightmare you had? Why do you think you had this nightmare?

Classbuilding Questions • © Kagan Publishing

18 | **GETTING TO KNOW YOU**

If you had to move to another country and live there for the rest of your life, which country would you choose and why?

Classbuilding Questions • © Kagan Publishing

19 | **GETTING TO KNOW YOU**

If you could give yourself a new first, middle, and last name, what would you name yourself? Explain your choices.

Classbuilding Questions • © Kagan Publishing

20 | **GETTING TO KNOW YOU**

What is the best thing about your neighborhood? What is the worst thing?

Classbuilding Questions • © Kagan Publishing

Classbuilding Questions
Kagan Publishing • (800) 933-2667 • www.KaganOnline.com

GETTING TO KNOW YOU
Journal Writing Question

What scares you? Tell about something that frightened you.

_____

_____

_____

_____

_____

_____

_____

_____

_____

_____

_____

_____

_____

_____

_____

_____

_____

_____

_____

_____

_____

GETTING TO KNOW YOU
Journal Writing Question

What are three positive qualities about you? Describe them in detail.

_____

_____

_____

_____

_____

_____

_____

_____

_____

_____

_____

_____

_____

_____

_____

_____

_____

Classbuilding Questions
Kagan Publishing • (800) 933-2667 • www.KaganOnline.com

card set
#**7**

GROWING UP

GROWING UP
Question Cards

① GROWING UP

How many kids are in your family? Where are you in the order? How many kids do you want and why?

Classbuilding Questions • © Kagan Publishing

② GROWING UP

Do you want to go to college? If yes, where and why? If no, why not?

Classbuilding Questions • © Kagan Publishing

③ GROWING UP

What do you want to do for a job when you grow up? What kind of education or training do you think you'll need for that?

Classbuilding Questions • © Kagan Publishing

④ GROWING UP

Do you want to be like your mom or dad when you grow up? Explain why or why not.

Classbuilding Questions • © Kagan Publishing

Classbuilding Questions
Kagan Publishing • (800) 933-2667 • www.KaganOnline.com

GROWING UP
Question Cards

5 GROWING UP

What are some things you can do now to make sure you are healthy when you get older? Explain.

Classbuilding Questions • © Kagan Publishing

6 GROWING UP

Do you know any kids that act more grown up than they are? How do they act? What do you think about their behavior? Explain.

Classbuilding Questions • © Kagan Publishing

7 GROWING UP

Do you know any grown-ups that act too young for their age? How do they act? What do you think about their behavior? Explain.

Classbuilding Questions • © Kagan Publishing

8 GROWING UP

What time in your life do you think is more fun? When you are a grown-up or while you are growing up? Explain.

Classbuilding Questions • © Kagan Publishing

GROWING UP
Question Cards

⑨ GROWING UP

Do you think the best days of your life are ahead of you or behind you? Explain.

Classbuilding Questions • © Kagan Publishing

⑩ GROWING UP

What are some things you believed as a kid that you no longer believe? What made you change the way you believe?

Classbuilding Questions • © Kagan Publishing

⑪ GROWING UP

What do you think is the best age? Kids, teenagers, or adults? Why?

Classbuilding Questions • © Kagan Publishing

⑫ GROWING UP

What is something that some grown-ups do that you'll never do when you grow up? Describe it.

Classbuilding Questions • © Kagan Publishing

GROWING UP
Question Cards

13 GROWING UP

How do you think you change physically as you grow up? How do you change mentally? What is the bigger change? Why?

Classbuilding Questions • © Kagan Publishing

14 GROWING UP

Wisdom comes with age. Do you agree or disagree? Explain.

Classbuilding Questions • © Kagan Publishing

15 GROWING UP

What does it mean to say, "Experience is the best teacher"?

Classbuilding Questions • © Kagan Publishing

16 GROWING UP

What scares you about getting older? Explain.

Classbuilding Questions • © Kagan Publishing

GROWING UP
Question Cards

---

17 | **GROWING UP**

How do you think your friendship choices might change as you grow up? Have you already experienced differences in how you select friends? What are they?

Classbuilding Questions • © Kagan Publishing

---

18 | **GROWING UP**

Do you think you will want more independence from your parents? How do you think your relationship with them will change as you grow older?

Classbuilding Questions • © Kagan Publishing

---

19 | **GROWING UP**

What do you look forward to about getting older? Why?

Classbuilding Questions • © Kagan Publishing

---

20 | **GROWING UP**

People develop at their own speed. Would you rather be an early bloomer or a late bloomer? Explain why.

Classbuilding Questions • © Kagan Publishing

Classbuilding Questions
Kagan Publishing • (800) 933-2667 • www.KaganOnline.com

GROWING UP
Journal Writing Question

How many kids are in your family? Where are you in the order? How many kids do you want and why?

_____

_____

_____

_____

_____

_____

_____

_____

_____

_____

_____

_____

_____

_____

_____

_____

_____

GROWING UP
Journal Writing Question

What do you want to do for a job when you grow up? What kind of education or training do you think you'll need for that?

_____

_____

_____

_____

_____

_____

_____

_____

_____

_____

_____

_____

_____

_____

_____

_____

_____

_____

Classbuilding Questions
Kagan Publishing • (800) 933-2667 • www.KaganOnline.com

card set
#**8**

HALLOWEEN

HALLOWEEN
Question Cards

HALLOWEEN

1

What is the scariest haunted house you've ever been in? Describe it.

Classbuilding Questions • © Kagan Publishing

HALLOWEEN

2

Is your neighborhood a good one for trick-or-treating? Why or why not? If not, what do you do?

Classbuilding Questions • © Kagan Publishing

HALLOWEEN

3

Does your family have any Halloween traditions? If yes, describe them. If no, what traditions would you like to start?

Classbuilding Questions • © Kagan Publishing

HALLOWEEN

4

Do you prefer store-bought costumes or original costumes people make? Explain why. Describe some you've seen that have been very creative.

Classbuilding Questions • © Kagan Publishing

Classbuilding Questions
Kagan Publishing • (800) 933-2667 • www.KaganOnline.com

HALLOWEEN
Question Cards

HALLOWEEN

5 What was your best Halloween ever? Describe it.

Classbuilding Questions • © Kagan Publishing

HALLOWEEN

6 How does your family usually decorate for Halloween? Describe.

Classbuilding Questions • © Kagan Publishing

HALLOWEEN

7 What is the best pumpkin you've ever carved or seen? Describe it.

Classbuilding Questions • © Kagan Publishing

HALLOWEEN

8 What are your favorite candies and treats to get on Halloween? Which are your least favorites? Why?

Classbuilding Questions • © Kagan Publishing

HALLOWEEN
Question Cards

HALLOWEEN
9

If you were going to have a Halloween party, how would you decorate? What would you do?

Classbuilding Questions • © Kagan Publishing

HALLOWEEN
10

If you were going to design the official logo for Halloween, what symbols and colors would you put on it and why?

Classbuilding Questions • © Kagan Publishing

HALLOWEEN
11

Do you believe in ghosts? Why or why not? Describe a personal experience if you've had one.

Classbuilding Questions • © Kagan Publishing

HALLOWEEN
12

Halloween is the best holiday of the year. Do you agree or disagree? Explain.

Classbuilding Questions • © Kagan Publishing

Classbuilding Questions
Kagan Publishing • (800) 933-2667 • www.KaganOnline.com

HALLOWEEN
Question Cards

---

(13) **HALLOWEEN**

If you got invited to a costume party and didn't have a costume yet, what costume could you put together using clothes and items you already have? Describe it.

Classbuilding Questions • © Kagan Publishing

---

(14) **HALLOWEEN**

What are some safety issues to keep in mind during Halloween? What can happen if you're not careful?

Classbuilding Questions • © Kagan Publishing

---

(15) **HALLOWEEN**

What do you think about kids who play pranks and do mischief around Halloween? What kind of pranks have you seen or done and how do you feel about them?

Classbuilding Questions • © Kagan Publishing

---

(16) **HALLOWEEN**

At what age are children old enough to go trick-or-treating without adult supervision? Why do you feel this way?

Classbuilding Questions • © Kagan Publishing

HALLOWEEN
Question Cards

HALLOWEEN

17

Have you ever been to a pumpkin patch to pick out a pumpkin and/or to do other activities? If yes, describe it. If no, to what kind of pumpkin patch would you want to go?

Classbuilding Questions • © Kagan Publishing

HALLOWEEN

18

Which of these Halloween characters do you like best and why: Dracula, werewolf, witch, Frankenstein, ghost? How would you dress up to be that character?

Classbuilding Questions • © Kagan Publishing

HALLOWEEN

19

What is the best-decorated house you've ever seen for Halloween? Describe it.

Classbuilding Questions • © Kagan Publishing

HALLOWEEN

20

Do you like to hand out candy? Why or why not?

Classbuilding Questions • © Kagan Publishing

HALLOWEEN
Journal Writing Question

What was your best Halloween ever? Describe it.

_____

_____

_____

_____

_____

_____

_____

_____

_____

_____

_____

_____

_____

_____

_____

_____

_____

_____

HALLOWEEN
Journal Writing Question

What is the scariest haunted house you've ever been in? Describe it.

_____

_____

_____

_____

_____

_____

_____

_____

_____

_____

_____

_____

_____

_____

_____

_____

_____

_____

_____

Classbuilding Questions
Kagan Publishing • (800) 933-2667 • www.KaganOnline.com

card set
#9

ICEBREAKERS

ICEBREAKERS
Question Cards

1 **ICEBREAKERS**

Have you ever been out of the country? If so, where's the best place you've been? If not, where would you want to go and why?

Classbuilding Questions • © Kagan Publishing

2 **ICEBREAKERS**

What is your favorite water sport and why?

Classbuilding Questions • © Kagan Publishing

3 **ICEBREAKERS**

Do you have a nickname? If yes, what is it? How did you get it? If no, what nickname would you like? Why?

Classbuilding Questions • © Kagan Publishing

4 **ICEBREAKERS**

Have you played on any sports teams? If yes, describe. If no, what team would you like to play on and why?

Classbuilding Questions • © Kagan Publishing

Classbuilding Questions
Kagan Publishing • (800) 933-2667 • www.KaganOnline.com

ICEBREAKERS
Question Cards

---

5 **ICEBREAKERS**

Have you ever taken any kind of lessons? If yes, describe. If no, what kind of lessons would you like to take on and why?

---

6 **ICEBREAKERS**

What is your favorite dinner? Describe it.

---

7 **ICEBREAKERS**

What is the best book you've read? Describe it.

---

8 **ICEBREAKERS**

Do you have any special talents or skills? What are they?

ICEBREAKERS
Question Cards

⑨ ICEBREAKERS

Can you cook? If yes, what do you cook? If not, how do you think you could learn?

Classbuilding Questions • © Kagan Publishing

⑩ ICEBREAKERS

What is the coolest thing you've ever built or created? Describe it.

Classbuilding Questions • © Kagan Publishing

⑪ ICEBREAKERS

What is your favorite kind of video game to play? Why?

Classbuilding Questions • © Kagan Publishing

⑫ ICEBREAKERS

Do you like to dance? If yes, describe your favorite kind of dancing. If no, why not?

Classbuilding Questions • © Kagan Publishing

Classbuilding Questions
Kagan Publishing • (800) 933-2667 • www.KaganOnline.com

ICEBREAKERS
Question Cards

13 ICEBREAKERS

Are you more of a social butterfly or a lone wolf? Explain.

Classbuilding Questions • © Kagan Publishing

14 ICEBREAKERS

Do you collect anything? If yes, describe. If no, what would you most likely collect? Why?

Classbuilding Questions • © Kagan Publishing

15 ICEBREAKERS

What is the most adventurous thing you've done? Explain.

Classbuilding Questions • © Kagan Publishing

16 ICEBREAKERS

Have you ever played an instrument? If yes, describe it. If no, which instrument would you most want to play? Why?

Classbuilding Questions • © Kagan Publishing

ICEBREAKERS
Question Cards

17 ICEBREAKERS

Would you want to be famous? If yes, what for? If no, why not?

Classbuilding Questions • © Kagan Publishing

18 ICEBREAKERS

How would you describe your perfect day?

Classbuilding Questions • © Kagan Publishing

19 ICEBREAKERS

What is one of the things you just couldn't live without and why?

Classbuilding Questions • © Kagan Publishing

20 ICEBREAKERS

What is one thing others don't know about you? Explain.

Classbuilding Questions • © Kagan Publishing

Classbuilding Questions
Kagan Publishing • (800) 933-2667 • www.KaganOnline.com

ICEBREAKERS
Journal Writing Question

Do you have a nickname? If yes, what is it? How did you get it? If no, what nickname would you like? Why?

_____

_____

_____

_____

_____

_____

_____

_____

_____

_____

_____

_____

_____

_____

_____

_____

_____

ICEBREAKERS
Journal Writing Question

What is one of the things you just couldn't live without and why?

_____

_____

_____

_____

_____

_____

_____

_____

_____

_____

_____

_____

_____

_____

_____

_____

Classbuilding Questions
Kagan Publishing • (800) 933-2667 • www.KaganOnline.com

IF...

IF...
Question Cards

1   **IF...**

If you were in the circus, what would be your role? Why would you choose this role?

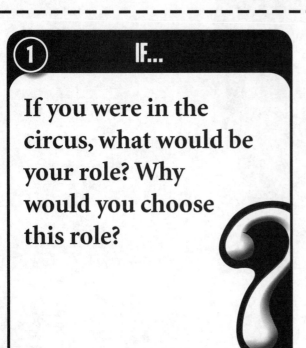

Classbuilding Questions • © Kagan Publishing

2   **IF...**

If you were going to write a book, what would you write about? Why this topic?

Classbuilding Questions • © Kagan Publishing

3   **IF...**

If you had to be stuck in an elevator with someone all day, who would it be? What would you do while stuck in there?

Classbuilding Questions • © Kagan Publishing

4   **IF...**

If you could be any famous athlete, who would you be and why?

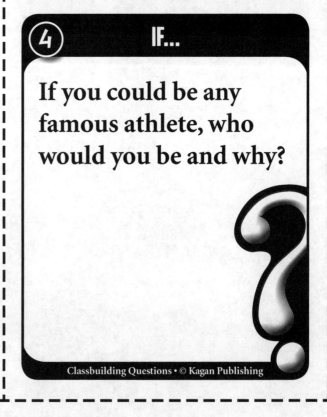

Classbuilding Questions • © Kagan Publishing

Classbuilding Questions
Kagan Publishing • (800) 933-2667 • www.KaganOnline.com

IF...
Question Cards

5 | IF...

If an alien offered to take you to space but said you could never return to earth would you go? Explain your answer.

Classbuilding Questions • © Kagan Publishing

6 | IF...

If you had to lose one of your senses, which one would you choose? Explain.

Classbuilding Questions • © Kagan Publishing

7 | IF...

If you had the power to fly or turn invisible, which would you choose and why?

Classbuilding Questions • © Kagan Publishing

8 | IF...

If you could do anything you wanted to tomorrow, what would you choose? Why?

Classbuilding Questions • © Kagan Publishing

IF...
Question Cards

9   **IF...**

If you could live forever, would you want to? Explain.

Classbuilding Questions • © Kagan Publishing

10   **IF...**

If you could go back into the past and change one thing, what would you change? Why this?

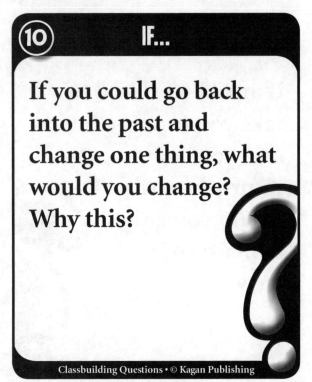

Classbuilding Questions • © Kagan Publishing

11   **IF...**

If you could travel in time, where and when would you go? Explain.

Classbuilding Questions • © Kagan Publishing

12   **IF...**

If you had to spend one million dollars in one day, what would you spend it on? Describe.

Classbuilding Questions • © Kagan Publishing

Classbuilding Questions
Kagan Publishing • (800) 933-2667 • www.KaganOnline.com

IF...
Question Cards

13 IF...

If you could open the restaurant, what would you call it, what would you serve, and how would it look? Why would you choose this theme?

14 IF...

If you could be five years older, would you be willing to skip those five years of your life? If yes, how do you think you would be different now? If not, why not?

15 IF...

If your dad offered to take you skydiving tomorrow, would you go? Why or why not?

16 IF...

If you could invent your own roller coaster, what would it be like? Describe it.

IF...
Question Cards

17   **IF...**

If you could spend a week's vacation anywhere in the world, where would you go and what would you do? Why do you choose this place?

Classbuilding Questions • © Kagan Publishing

18   **IF...**

If you could solve one world problem, what would you solve and why?

Classbuilding Questions • © Kagan Publishing

19   **IF...**

If you had a weather machine that could change the weather, what would you do with it?

Classbuilding Questions • © Kagan Publishing

20   **IF...**

If a genie granted you one wish, what would you wish for and why?

Classbuilding Questions • © Kagan Publishing

94

IF...
Journal Writing Question

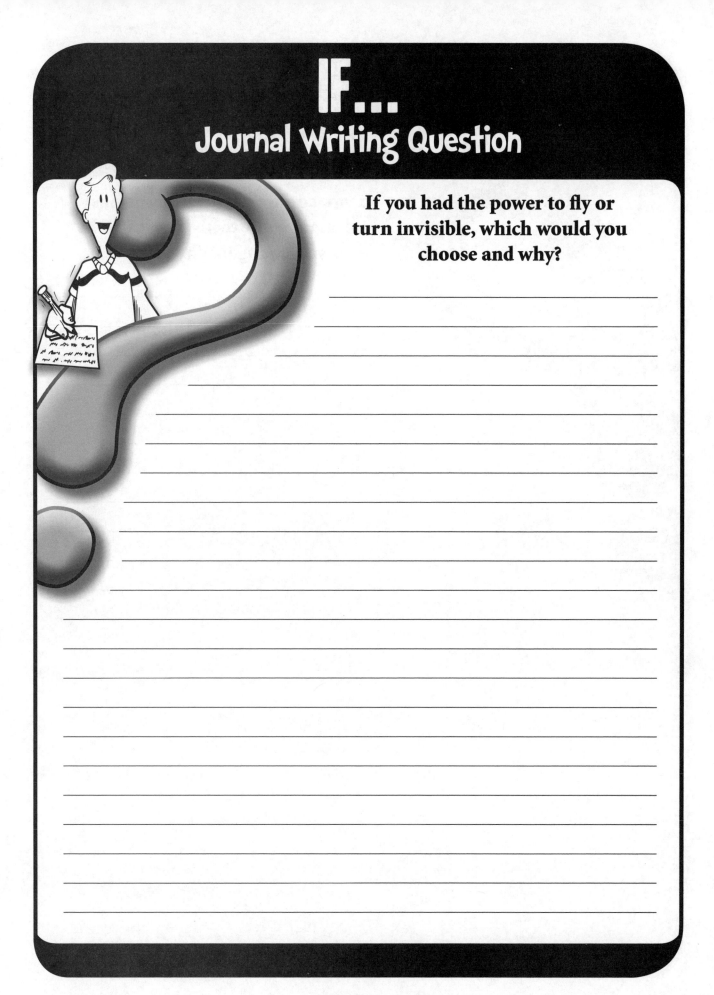

If you had the power to fly or turn invisible, which would you choose and why?

_____

_____

_____

_____

_____

_____

_____

_____

_____

_____

_____

_____

_____

_____

_____

_____

_____

_____

IF...
Journal Writing Question

If you could go back into the past and change one thing, what would you change? Why this?

_____

_____

_____

_____

_____

_____

_____

_____

_____

_____

_____

_____

_____

_____

_____

_____

_____

_____

_____

Classbuilding Questions
Kagan Publishing • (800) 933-2667 • www.KaganOnline.com

MAKE A LIST

MAKE A LIST
Question Cards

---

① MAKE A LIST

Make a list of cereal flavors you know. Which is your favorite and why?

Classbuilding Questions • © Kagan Publishing

---

② MAKE A LIST

Make a list of ice cream flavors you like. Which is your favorite and why?

Classbuilding Questions • © Kagan Publishing

---

③ MAKE A LIST

Make a list of movies you've seen. Which ones would you see again? Why?

Classbuilding Questions • © Kagan Publishing

---

④ MAKE A LIST

Make a list of television shows for kids that you like to watch. What makes you choose these shows? Explain.

Classbuilding Questions • © Kagan Publishing

MAKE A LIST
Question Cards

---

(5) MAKE A LIST

Make a list of holidays you celebrate. Who do you celebrate with and what do you do?

Classbuilding Questions • © Kagan Publishing

---

(6) MAKE A LIST

Make a list of places you'd like to travel to. How did you choose these places?

Classbuilding Questions • © Kagan Publishing

---

(7) MAKE A LIST

Make a list of animals you like. Can you name some of the characteristics of one or two?

Classbuilding Questions • © Kagan Publishing

---

(8) MAKE A LIST

Make a list of toys you've owned. What was your favorite toy of all time? Why?

Classbuilding Questions • © Kagan Publishing

MAKE A LIST
Question Cards

⑨ MAKE A LIST

Make a list of games you like to play. What types of games do you like best? Describe one of these.

Classbuilding Questions • © Kagan Publishing

⑩ MAKE A LIST

Make a list of amusement park rides you love. How are the rides alike and different?

Classbuilding Questions • © Kagan Publishing

⑪ MAKE A LIST

Make a list of cartoons you watch. Why do you watch these instead of others?

Classbuilding Questions • © Kagan Publishing

⑫ MAKE A LIST

Make a list of superheroes. Which one would you be if you could be a superhero? Why?

Classbuilding Questions • © Kagan Publishing

Classbuilding Questions
Kagan Publishing • (800) 933-2667 • www.KaganOnline.com

MAKE A LIST
Question Cards

---

13 — MAKE A LIST

Make a list of sports you like to play. Which of these sports do you play most frequently? What do you like about them?

Classbuilding Questions • © Kagan Publishing

---

14 — MAKE A LIST

Make a list of teachers you've had. Who was your favorite teacher? Why?

Classbuilding Questions • © Kagan Publishing

---

15 — MAKE A LIST

Make a list of restaurants where you like to eat. Which one serves you the food you like most? How often do you eat there?

Classbuilding Questions • © Kagan Publishing

---

16 — MAKE A LIST

Make a list of your favorite drinks. Are you allowed to drink these anytime you want to or are they reserved for special occasions? Which drinks and occasions?

Classbuilding Questions • © Kagan Publishing

MAKE A LIST
Question Cards

17 MAKE A LIST

Make a list of video games you like to play. Which one is your favorite and why?

18 MAKE A LIST

Make a list of things you could do on a rainy day. What makes a rainy day special for doing things you don't usually do? Explain.

19 MAKE A LIST

Make a list of your favorite desserts. How would you describe it on a restaurant menu to make it sound appetizing?

20 MAKE A LIST

Make a list of healthy snacks you can eat. Do you think healthy snacks are a better choice than junk foods and sweets? Explain.

Classbuilding Questions
Kagan Publishing • (800) 933-2667 • www.KaganOnline.com

MAKE A LIST
Journal Writing Question

Make a list of television shows for kids that you like to watch. What makes you choose these shows? Explain.

_____

_____

_____

_____

_____

_____

_____

_____

_____

_____

_____

_____

_____

_____

_____

_____

_____

MAKE A LIST
Journal Writing Question

Make a list of things you could do on a rainy day. What makes a rainy day special for doing things you don't usually do? Explain.

_____

_____

_____

_____

_____

_____

_____

_____

_____

_____

_____

_____

_____

_____

_____

_____

_____

Classbuilding Questions
Kagan Publishing • (800) 933-2667 • www.KaganOnline.com

PETS

PETS
Question Cards

PETS

1 Do you have any pets? If so, what kind of pets do you have? How did you get your pet? If not, what pet would you like to have and why?

Classbuilding Questions • © Kagan Publishing

PETS

2 Would you rather have a dog, cat, hamster, or fish? Why?

Classbuilding Questions • © Kagan Publishing

PETS

3 Pick one pet and describe its personality. If you don't have a pet, describe the personality of the pet you'd like to have.

Classbuilding Questions • © Kagan Publishing

PETS

4 Describe one funny behavior of your pet. When does your pet display this behavior?

Classbuilding Questions • © Kagan Publishing

Classbuilding Questions
Kagan Publishing • (800) 933-2667 • www.KaganOnline.com

PETS

Question Cards

PETS

5

It should be illegal to have wild animals as pets, such as tigers and ferrets. Do you agree or disagree? Why?

Classbuilding Questions • © Kagan Publishing

PETS

6

What do you think is the easiest pet to maintain? Why?

Classbuilding Questions • © Kagan Publishing

PETS

7

If you found a dog in your front yard without a collar, what would you do? Explain.

Classbuilding Questions • © Kagan Publishing

PETS

8

If the family dog bit one of the kids, what should the family do with the dog? Explain.

Classbuilding Questions • © Kagan Publishing

PETS
Question Cards

PETS ⑨

If your dog chewed up the brand-new toy you received for your birthday, what would you do? Explain.

Classbuilding Questions • © Kagan Publishing

PETS ⑩

Should a limit be set as to the number of pets one person or one family can own? Why or why not?

Classbuilding Questions • © Kagan Publishing

PETS ⑪

Would you want to be a vet? Why or why not?

Classbuilding Questions • © Kagan Publishing

PETS ⑫

Do you think animals have feelings? Explain your answer.

Classbuilding Questions • © Kagan Publishing

Classbuilding Questions
Kagan Publishing • (800) 933-2667 • www.KaganOnline.com

PETS

Question Cards

PETS (13)

Do you think pets need to be disciplined? What is the appropriate punishment for a pet? What is inappropriate? Explain.

Classbuilding Questions • © Kagan Publishing

PETS (14)

Are pets members of the family? Explain your answer.

Classbuilding Questions • © Kagan Publishing

PETS (15)

Pets can be very expensive. How so?

Classbuilding Questions • © Kagan Publishing

PETS (16)

How important is it to research the type of pet you want to own? Name some things you should consider before you acquire a pet.

Classbuilding Questions • © Kagan Publishing

PETS
Question Cards

PETS 17

Many animals are used for service. Is training a dog for service different from training it for a pet? How? Name some ways that animals help people and organizations?

Classbuilding Questions • © Kagan Publishing

PETS 18

What are the most important training lessons you can give your pet? Describe them. Why do think it is important to train a pet? Explain.

Classbuilding Questions • © Kagan Publishing

PETS 19

If you have a pet in your family, what are your responsibilities in taking care of it? If not, what do you think your duties should be? Explain why.

Classbuilding Questions • © Kagan Publishing

PETS 20

Have you ever volunteered to work at an animal shelter? If yes, describe your experience. If you volunteered, what could you do?

Classbuilding Questions • © Kagan Publishing

Classbuilding Questions
Kagan Publishing • (800) 933-2667 • www.KaganOnline.com

PETS
Journal Writing Question

Describe one funny behavior of your pet. When does your pet display this behavior?

_____

_____

_____

_____

_____

_____

_____

_____

_____

_____

_____

_____

_____

_____

_____

_____

PETS
Journal Writing Question

How important is it to research the type of pet you want to own? Name some things you should consider before you acquire a pet.

_____

_____

_____

_____

_____

_____

_____

_____

_____

_____

_____

_____

_____

_____

_____

_____

_____

Classbuilding Questions
Kagan Publishing • (800) 933-2667 • www.KaganOnline.com

card set
#**13**

SCHOOL DAYS

SCHOOL DAYS
Question Cards

1 **SCHOOL DAYS**

What is your favorite subject and why?

Classbuilding Questions • © Kagan Publishing

1 **SCHOOL DAYS**

What is your favorite subject and why?

Classbuilding Questions • © Kagan Publishing

2 **SCHOOL DAYS**

Why is a good education important? Explain.

Classbuilding Questions • © Kagan Publishing

3 **SCHOOL DAYS**

If you could change one thing about your school, what would it be? Why?

Classbuilding Questions • © Kagan Publishing

4 **SCHOOL DAYS**

What things are you really good at in school? Describe.

Classbuilding Questions • © Kagan Publishing

Classbuilding Questions
Kagan Publishing • (800) 933-2667 • www.KaganOnline.com

SCHOOL DAYS
Question Cards

⑤ SCHOOL DAYS

What is your daily routine before school? Describe what you do.

Classbuilding Questions • © Kagan Publishing

⑥ SCHOOL DAYS

How important are grades to you? Explain why they are important.

Classbuilding Questions • © Kagan Publishing

⑦ SCHOOL DAYS

Who is your biggest cheerleader for your education? Why?

Classbuilding Questions • © Kagan Publishing

⑧ SCHOOL DAYS

Who was your favorite teacher and why? What qualities set this teacher apart from others? Explain.

Classbuilding Questions • © Kagan Publishing

SCHOOL DAYS
Question Cards

⑨ SCHOOL DAYS

What are you really proud about in school? Describe.

Classbuilding Questions • © Kagan Publishing

⑩ SCHOOL DAYS

Why do you think kids are required to go to school? What would you do if it was your choice?

Classbuilding Questions • © Kagan Publishing

⑪ SCHOOL DAYS

Would you rather have many short breaks or one long summer break? Why or why not?

Classbuilding Questions • © Kagan Publishing

⑫ SCHOOL DAYS

Would you like to be homeschooled? What do you think could be the advantages? What are the disadvantages?

Classbuilding Questions • © Kagan Publishing

Classbuilding Questions
Kagan Publishing • (800) 933-2667 • www.KaganOnline.com

SCHOOL DAYS
Question Cards

13 SCHOOL DAYS

What do you plan to do when you graduate? Explain.

Classbuilding Questions • © Kagan Publishing

14 SCHOOL DAYS

Do you prefer to work on your own or in small groups or teams? What are the benefits of each?

Classbuilding Questions • © Kagan Publishing

15 SCHOOL DAYS

How does school prepare you for the real world? Explain.

Classbuilding Questions • © Kagan Publishing

16 SCHOOL DAYS

What is one thing you learned that you'll never forget? How did you learn it?

Classbuilding Questions • © Kagan Publishing

SCHOOL DAYS
Question Cards

17 SCHOOL DAYS

If you could be a genius in one subject, what would it be and why?

Classbuilding Questions • © Kagan Publishing

18 SCHOOL DAYS

Would you get anything special if you had a perfect report card? If not, do you think you would still work as hard? Explain.

Classbuilding Questions • © Kagan Publishing

19 SCHOOL DAYS

How would you describe your study habits? If you need improvement, what steps could you take to get you on track now?

Classbuilding Questions • © Kagan Publishing

20 SCHOOL DAYS

What's more important to you: learning or grades? Explain the difference.

Classbuilding Questions • © Kagan Publishing

Classbuilding Questions
Kagan Publishing • (800) 933-2667 • www.KaganOnline.com

SCHOOL DAYS
Journal Writing Question

Who was your favorite teacher and why? What qualities set this teacher apart from others? Explain.

_____

_____

_____

_____

_____

_____

_____

_____

_____

_____

_____

_____

_____

_____

_____

_____

_____

_____

SCHOOL DAYS
Journal Writing Question

What are you really proud about in school? Describe.

_____

_____

_____

_____

_____

_____

_____

_____

_____

_____

_____

_____

_____

_____

_____

_____

_____

Classbuilding Questions
Kagan Publishing • (800) 933-2667 • www.KaganOnline.com

card set
#14

SHOPPING

SHOPPING
Question Cards

SHOPPING

1 SHOPPING

What is your favorite store and why?

Classbuilding Questions • © Kagan Publishing

2 SHOPPING

Do you like shopping? Why or why not?

Classbuilding Questions • © Kagan Publishing

3 SHOPPING

What is the last thing someone bought for you? Did you like it? Describe it.

Classbuilding Questions • © Kagan Publishing

4 SHOPPING

Do you like to go into the store and get exactly what you need and get out, or do you like to take your time and look around before you buy? Explain.

Classbuilding Questions • © Kagan Publishing

Classbuilding Questions
Kagan Publishing • (800) 933-2667 • www.KaganOnline.com

SHOPPING
Question Cards

⑤ SHOPPING

How do you earn money to go shopping? Describe.

Classbuilding Questions • © Kagan Publishing

⑥ SHOPPING

In which type of store would you rather have a shopping spree: A clothing store, game store, or sporting goods store? Why?

Classbuilding Questions • © Kagan Publishing

⑦ SHOPPING

If you went shopping in a bookstore, what would you do? Describe.

Classbuilding Questions • © Kagan Publishing

⑧ SHOPPING

Who do you know that loves to shop? Why do you think he or she likes shopping so much? What are the pitfalls of shopping too much?

Classbuilding Questions • © Kagan Publishing

SHOPPING
Question Cards

---

⑨ SHOPPING

There's a saying, "You get what you pay for." Do you think it's true that the more you pay, the better the item is? Explain.

---

⑩ SHOPPING

Do you consider yourself more of a saver or more of a spender? Why?

---

⑪ SHOPPING

Describe your last grocery shopping experience. What are your decisions and responsibilities when it comes to grocery shopping?

---

⑫ SHOPPING

If you were going to buy a gift for your best friend, what store would you go to and what would you get? Why?

SHOPPING
Question Cards

---

13 | **SHOPPING**

Do you like going to the mall? Why or why not? What do you do there?

Classbuilding Questions • © Kagan Publishing

---

14 | **SHOPPING**

Do you wait for a store to have a sale before you go shopping? How do you find out the store is having a sale?

Classbuilding Questions • © Kagan Publishing

---

15 | **SHOPPING**

Would you rather buy things on the Internet or go to a store to buy them? Explain.

Classbuilding Questions • © Kagan Publishing

---

16 | **SHOPPING**

How much does price influence your decisions? Explain a situation when this was true.

Classbuilding Questions • © Kagan Publishing

SHOPPING
Question Cards

---

17 **SHOPPING**

How important are name brands to you? Why or why not? Explain the differences.

Classbuilding Questions • © Kagan Publishing

---

18 **SHOPPING**

What kind of influences do TV commercials have on your buying habits? Give some examples. What are other influences?

Classbuilding Questions • © Kagan Publishing

---

19 **SHOPPING**

Do you think it is better to give than to receive? Why or why not?

Classbuilding Questions • © Kagan Publishing

---

20 **SHOPPING**

What are some occasions, other than birthdays, that you might need to buy gifts for others? Why do gifts mean so much? Explain.

Classbuilding Questions • © Kagan Publishing

SHOPPING
Journal Writing Question

In which type of store would you rather have a shopping spree: A clothing store, game store, or sporting goods store? Why?

_____

_____

_____

_____

_____

_____

_____

_____

_____

_____

_____

_____

_____

_____

_____

_____

SHOPPING
Journal Writing Question

What kind of influences do TV commercials have on your buying habits? Give some examples. What are other influences?

_____

_____

_____

_____

_____

_____

_____

_____

_____

_____

_____

_____

_____

_____

_____

_____

_____

_____

Classbuilding Questions
Kagan Publishing • (800) 933-2667 • www.KaganOnline.com

SPORTS

SPORTS
Question Cards

1 SPORTS

Do you prefer to play sports or watch sports? Describe.

Classbuilding Questions • © Kagan Publishing

2 SPORTS

Do you have any favorite sports teams? Name them. What makes them your favorites?

Classbuilding Questions • © Kagan Publishing

3 SPORTS

What are three sports that you enjoy playing? Why? What positions do you play?

Classbuilding Questions • © Kagan Publishing

4 SPORTS

What positive things do people learn from playing sports? Explain.

Classbuilding Questions • © Kagan Publishing

Classbuilding Questions
Kagan Publishing • (800) 933-2667 • www.KaganOnline.com

SPORTS
Question Cards

5 | SPORTS

Have you ever been to a professional game? Describe it. If not, which game would you love to see? Why?

Classbuilding Questions • © Kagan Publishing

6 | SPORTS

Do you prefer ball sports, or board sports? Explain.

Classbuilding Questions • © Kagan Publishing

7 | SPORTS

Have you ever done any extreme sports? What makes them extreme? If not, in what extreme sport would you like to participate?

Classbuilding Questions • © Kagan Publishing

8 | SPORTS

What things do you like about your favorite sport? Explain.

Classbuilding Questions • © Kagan Publishing

SPORTS
Question Cards

---

⑨ SPORTS

What professional team do you think has the coolest uniforms? Describe.

---

⑩ SPORTS

If you could switch places with one athlete for one day, who would you choose and why?

---

⑪ SPORTS

If you could have lunch with one famous athlete from the past, who would you choose? Why? What would you talk about?

---

⑫ SPORTS

What do you think is the hardest sport to play and why?

Classbuilding Questions
Kagan Publishing • (800) 933-2667 • www.KaganOnline.com

SPORTS
Question Cards

13 **SPORTS**

Do you have practice for any sports that you play? How often? Why do you think practices are important?

Classbuilding Questions • © Kagan Publishing

14 **SPORTS**

Who do you think is the best athlete in the world? Why?

Classbuilding Questions • © Kagan Publishing

15 **SPORTS**

It would take a lot of dedication and a lot of practice to be in the Olympics. Would you want to be in the Olympics? Explain why or why not.

Classbuilding Questions • © Kagan Publishing

16 **SPORTS**

What is your proudest sports accomplishment? Describe it.

Classbuilding Questions • © Kagan Publishing

SPORTS
Question Cards

17 SPORTS

Pick a sport you know the rules to and explain them to somebody who doesn't know them. Why is it important to understand the rules?

Classbuilding Questions • © Kagan Publishing

18 SPORTS

Have you ever been injured playing sports? Describe your worst injury. How can you avoid being injured? Explain some safety tips.

Classbuilding Questions • © Kagan Publishing

19 SPORTS

What does it mean to be a sore loser? Have you ever felt that way? Describe the incident and what you did.

Classbuilding Questions • © Kagan Publishing

20 SPORTS

What is the importance of good sportsmanship? Explain how it affects the entire team and the fans if poor sportsmanship is demonstrated.

Classbuilding Questions • © Kagan Publishing

Classbuilding Questions
Kagan Publishing • (800) 933-2667 • www.KaganOnline.com

SPORTS
Journal Writing Question

What positive things do people learn from playing sports? Explain.

_____

_____

_____

_____

_____

_____

_____

_____

_____

_____

_____

_____

_____

_____

_____

_____

SPORTS
Journal Writing Question

If you could have lunch with one famous athlete from the past, who would you choose? Why? What would you talk about?

_____

_____

_____

_____

_____

_____

_____

_____

_____

_____

_____

_____

_____

_____

_____

_____

Classbuilding Questions
Kagan Publishing • (800) 933-2667 • www.KaganOnline.com

card set
#**16**

TECHNOLOGY

TECHNOLOGY
Question Cards

---

1 TECHNOLOGY

How does technology help make you smarter? Explain.

Classbuilding Questions • © Kagan Publishing

---

2 TECHNOLOGY

List your top five favorite websites and why you like them. How do you use them? Explain.

Classbuilding Questions • © Kagan Publishing

---

3 TECHNOLOGY

Complete the following sentence. Technology is…

Classbuilding Questions • © Kagan Publishing

---

4 TECHNOLOGY

The Internet is the best invention of all time. Do you agree or disagree? Explain.

Classbuilding Questions • © Kagan Publishing

Classbuilding Questions
Kagan Publishing • (800) 933-2667 • www.KaganOnline.com

TECHNOLOGY
Question Cards

TECHNOLOGY

⑤ What changes in technology have you seen in your lifetime? Describe how they have affected your behavior.

Classbuilding Questions • © Kagan Publishing

TECHNOLOGY

⑥ Are humans smarter than computers or are computers smarter than humans? Explain.

Classbuilding Questions • © Kagan Publishing

TECHNOLOGY

⑦ How would you rate your computer skills on a scale of 1 to 10? Explain.

Classbuilding Questions • © Kagan Publishing

TECHNOLOGY

⑧ In what ways do you see technology making the world a better place?

Classbuilding Questions • © Kagan Publishing

TECHNOLOGY
Question Cards

TECHNOLOGY

9

What are the negatives of technology? How has technology influenced you unfavorably? Think carefully about this.

Classbuilding Questions • © Kagan Publishing

TECHNOLOGY

10

Technology has made the world smaller. Do you agree or disagree? Explain what this means.

Classbuilding Questions • © Kagan Publishing

TECHNOLOGY

11

Who is the most technological person you know? What does he or she do with technology? Explain.

Classbuilding Questions • © Kagan Publishing

TECHNOLOGY

12

Do you think the government should regulate the Internet? Why or why not? How could this change the way people get information? Explain.

Classbuilding Questions • © Kagan Publishing

Classbuilding Questions
Kagan Publishing • (800) 933-2667 • www.KaganOnline.com

TECHNOLOGY
Question Cards

TECHNOLOGY

13

Which technology companies do you like the best and why?

Classbuilding Questions • © Kagan Publishing

TECHNOLOGY

14

How long could you go without technology until you really started missing it? In what ways do you use it that you would miss it so much?

Classbuilding Questions • © Kagan Publishing

TECHNOLOGY

15

What is a better invention? The television, the telephone, the computer, or the Internet? Explain.

Classbuilding Questions • © Kagan Publishing

TECHNOLOGY

16

What kinds of science fiction have you seen in movies or read about in books that have actually become reality? How can you explain this?

Classbuilding Questions • © Kagan Publishing

TECHNOLOGY
Question Cards

TECHNOLOGY

17

Do you have any rules in your family for using the Internet? Why do you think it is important to have limits? Explain your answer.

Classbuilding Questions • © Kagan Publishing

TECHNOLOGY

18

What technologies are you personally dependent on in a good way? Which ones affect you in a bad way? Explain.

Classbuilding Questions • © Kagan Publishing

TECHNOLOGY

19

How do you think technology will affect your work life? Explain.

Classbuilding Questions • © Kagan Publishing

TECHNOLOGY

20

How has technology benefited medicine, space exploration, education and entertainment? Give some examples.

Classbuilding Questions • © Kagan Publishing

TECHNOLOGY
Journal Writing Question

What technologies are you personally dependent on in a good way? Which ones affect you in a bad way? Explain.

_____

_____

_____

_____

_____

_____

_____

_____

_____

_____

_____

_____

_____

_____

_____

_____

_____

TECHNOLOGY
Journal Writing Question

How has technology benefited medicine, space exploration, education and entertainment? Give some examples.

_____

_____

_____

_____

_____

_____

_____

_____

_____

_____

_____

_____

_____

_____

_____

_____

_____

_____

_____

_____

Classbuilding Questions
Kagan Publishing • (800) 933-2667 • www.KaganOnline.com

card set
#17

TELEVISION

TELEVISION
Question Cards

1 TELEVISION

How would you describe your favorite television show to somebody who has never seen it?

Classbuilding Questions • © Kagan Publishing

2 TELEVISION

Do you think there should be a limit to how much TV a person should be able to watch every day? Defend your answer.

Classbuilding Questions • © Kagan Publishing

3 TELEVISION

What are three shows on TV that you love to watch? Why?

Classbuilding Questions • © Kagan Publishing

4 TELEVISION

What is the funniest show on TV that you watch? What makes it so funny?

Classbuilding Questions • © Kagan Publishing

Classbuilding Questions
Kagan Publishing • (800) 933-2667 • www.KaganOnline.com

TELEVISION
Question Cards

5 **TELEVISION**

Do you prefer television shows or movies? Why?

Classbuilding Questions • © Kagan Publishing

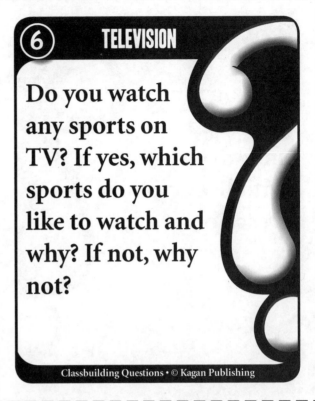

6 **TELEVISION**

Do you watch any sports on TV? If yes, which sports do you like to watch and why? If not, why not?

Classbuilding Questions • © Kagan Publishing

7 **TELEVISION**

Time spent watching TV is wasted time. Do you agree or disagree? Why?

Classbuilding Questions • © Kagan Publishing

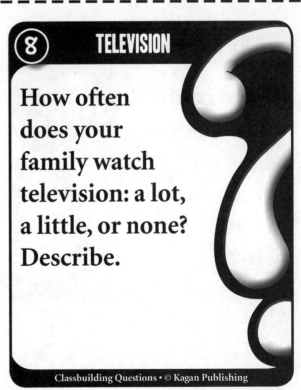

8 **TELEVISION**

How often does your family watch television: a lot, a little, or none? Describe.

Classbuilding Questions • © Kagan Publishing

TELEVISION
Question Cards

9 TELEVISION

Do you prefer animated shows or shows with live actors? Describe.

10 TELEVISION

Do you think it's a problem to watch too much TV? What are some of the signs that you have? How do you feel? Explain.

11 TELEVISION

If you could only see one show on TV, which show would it be and why?

12 TELEVISION

Do your parents limit what types of shows you can watch? What shows are you not allowed to watch and why?

Classbuilding Questions
Kagan Publishing • (800) 933-2667 • www.KaganOnline.com

TELEVISION
Question Cards

13 TELEVISION

Do you think watching violent TV shows makes people more violent? Explain.

Classbuilding Questions • © Kagan Publishing

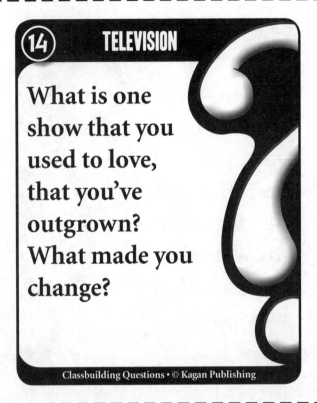

14 TELEVISION

What is one show that you used to love, that you've outgrown? What made you change?

Classbuilding Questions • © Kagan Publishing

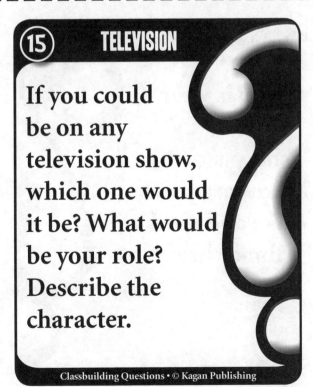

15 TELEVISION

If you could be on any television show, which one would it be? What would be your role? Describe the character.

Classbuilding Questions • © Kagan Publishing

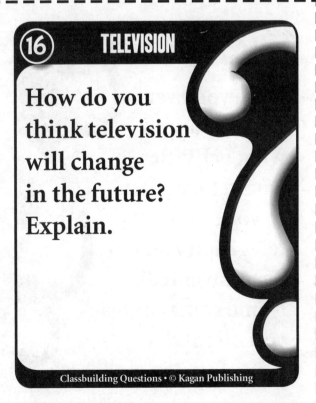

16 TELEVISION

How do you think television will change in the future? Explain.

Classbuilding Questions • © Kagan Publishing

TELEVISION
Question Cards

17 TELEVISION

Do you have a television in your room? If yes, what rules do you follow for watching? Explain. If no, why not?

Classbuilding Questions • © Kagan Publishing

18 TELEVISION

Do you prefer a comedy or drama? Do you think that says anything about you as a person? Explain.

Classbuilding Questions • © Kagan Publishing

19 TELEVISION

Have you ever thought about what activities would take place in your home if television had not been invented? Name some things you might do.

Classbuilding Questions • © Kagan Publishing

20 TELEVISION

Who is your favorite TV show actor? How are you like and unlike him or her?

Classbuilding Questions • © Kagan Publishing

Classbuilding Questions
Kagan Publishing • (800) 933-2667 • www.KaganOnline.com

TELEVISION
Journal Writing Question

How would you describe your favorite television show to somebody who has never seen it?

_____

_____

_____

_____

_____

_____

_____

_____

_____

_____

_____

_____

_____

_____

_____

_____

_____

_____

_____

TELEVISION
Journal Writing Question

If you could be on any television show, which one would it be? What would be your role? Describe the character.

_____

_____

_____

_____

_____

_____

_____

_____

_____

_____

_____

_____

_____

_____

_____

_____

_____

_____

Classbuilding Questions
Kagan Publishing • (800) 933-2667 • www.KaganOnline.com

card set
#18

THANKSGIVING

THANKSGIVING
Question Cards

1 **THANKSGIVING**

Thanksgiving is a time for giving thanks. What are you most thankful for and why?

Classbuilding Questions • © Kagan Publishing

2 **THANKSGIVING**

What is your favorite Thanksgiving dish? Describe it.

Classbuilding Questions • © Kagan Publishing

3 **THANKSGIVING**

What Thanksgiving traditions does your family have? If you can't think of any, which traditions would you like to have?

Classbuilding Questions • © Kagan Publishing

4 **THANKSGIVING**

What do you look forward to most about Thanksgiving? Describe.

Classbuilding Questions • © Kagan Publishing

Classbuilding Questions
Kagan Publishing • (800) 933-2667 • www.KaganOnline.com

THANKSGIVING
Question Cards

5 THANKSGIVING

How could you explain why we celebrate Thanksgiving to someone from another culture that doesn't celebrate it?

Classbuilding Questions • © Kagan Publishing

6 THANKSGIVING

The turducken is a chicken stuffed into a duck, which then is stuffed into a turkey. Invent a Thanksgiving Day dish and give it a name.

Classbuilding Questions • © Kagan Publishing

7 THANKSGIVING

What is your best Thanksgiving memory? Describe it.

Classbuilding Questions • © Kagan Publishing

8 THANKSGIVING

Do you have a job or responsibility for Thanksgiving? If so, what is it? If not, what job could you take on? Explain.

Classbuilding Questions • © Kagan Publishing

THANKSGIVING
Question Cards

⑨ THANKSGIVING

What do you know about the history of Thanksgiving? Explain. What more would you like to know? Give details.

Classbuilding Questions • © Kagan Publishing

⑩ THANKSGIVING

If you were in charge of creating a Thanksgiving Day parade, what would you plan for the parade? Describe what it would look like, sound like, and what would happen.

Classbuilding Questions • © Kagan Publishing

⑪ THANKSGIVING

Do sports play a role in your family on Thanksgiving Day? If yes, Describe. If not, in what other activity does the family participate?

Classbuilding Questions • © Kagan Publishing

⑫ THANKSGIVING

Thanksgiving is often considered family time. With which family members do you get together ? What do you do?

Classbuilding Questions • © Kagan Publishing

Classbuilding Questions
Kagan Publishing • (800) 933-2667 • www.KaganOnline.com

13 **THANKSGIVING**

If you were going to make a wish using the turkey wishbone, what would you wish for and why?

Classbuilding Questions • © Kagan Publishing

14 **THANKSGIVING**

The U.S. President traditionally "pardons" the National Thanksgiving Turkey, allowing it to live the rest of its life on the farm instead of being turned into a turkey dinner. What are your feelings about this tradition?

Classbuilding Questions • © Kagan Publishing

15 **THANKSGIVING**

Does it matter to you how turkeys are treated if they are going to be slaughtered for food anyway? Explain how you feel about this.

Classbuilding Questions • © Kagan Publishing

16 **THANKSGIVING**

The famous Thanksgiving story tells of 'Pilgrims and Indians' sharing a feast of harvest after the American Indians taught the Pilgrims to fish and farm. Why do you think so much conflict existed between the Native Americans and settlers?

Classbuilding Questions • © Kagan Publishing

THANKSGIVING
Question Cards

17 THANKSGIVING

Ben Franklin wanted the turkey to be the national bird of the United States. Do you think the turkey is a good national bird? Why or why not? What other bird do you think is a better national bird? Why?

Classbuilding Questions • © Kagan Publishing

18 THANKSGIVING

Many families play games during Thanksgiving. What board, card, or other games does your family play during Thanksgiving? If you don't play, which games would you like to play?

Classbuilding Questions • © Kagan Publishing

19 THANKSGIVING

Many people in our country can't afford to celebrate Thanksgiving Day with a turkey and all the trimmings. What could you do to help? Describe.

Classbuilding Questions • © Kagan Publishing

20 THANKSGIVING

Why were Pilgrims in America happy just to survive? How is their life different from your life today? Explain.

Classbuilding Questions • © Kagan Publishing

Classbuilding Questions
Kagan Publishing • (800) 933-2667 • www.KaganOnline.com

THANKSGIVING
Journal Writing Question

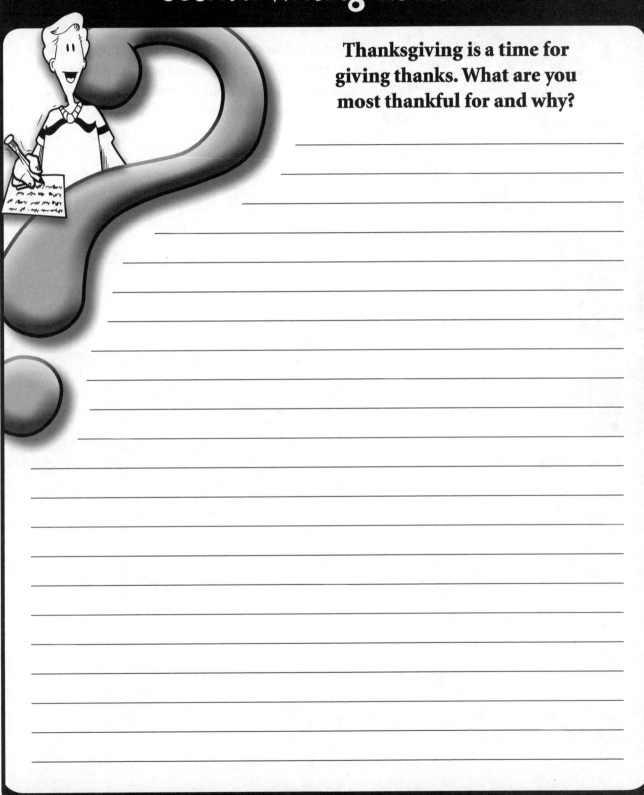

Thanksgiving is a time for giving thanks. What are you most thankful for and why?

_____

_____

_____

_____

_____

_____

_____

_____

_____

_____

_____

_____

_____

_____

_____

_____

_____

_____

_____

THANKSGIVING
Journal Writing Question

If you were in charge of creating a Thanksgiving Day parade, what would you plan for the parade? Describe what it would look like, sound like, and what would happen.

_____

_____

_____

_____

_____

_____

_____

_____

_____

_____

_____

_____

_____

_____

_____

_____

Classbuilding Questions
Kagan Publishing • (800) 933-2667 • www.KaganOnline.com

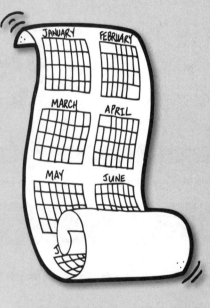

TODAY

TODAY

Question Cards

1 TODAY

What have you eaten today? Describe it in detail.

Classbuilding Questions • © Kagan Publishing

2 TODAY

Who have you interacted with today and about what?

Classbuilding Questions • © Kagan Publishing

3 TODAY

What has been the best part of your day so far? Describe it and why.

Classbuilding Questions • © Kagan Publishing

4 TODAY

What's the hardest thing you had to do today so far? Describe it.

Classbuilding Questions • © Kagan Publishing

Classbuilding Questions
Kagan Publishing • (800) 933-2667 • www.KaganOnline.com

TODAY
Question Cards

5 **TODAY**

What have you learned today? Describe it in detail.

Classbuilding Questions • © Kagan Publishing

6 **TODAY**

What time did you wake up this morning? How do you usually wake up? Is it easy or difficult? Describe the schedule.

Classbuilding Questions • © Kagan Publishing

7 **TODAY**

Did you get enough sleep last night? Explain why it is important to get sufficient sleep each night.

Classbuilding Questions • © Kagan Publishing

8 **TODAY**

How is today different from any other day? Explain.

Classbuilding Questions • © Kagan Publishing

 **TODAY**

Question Cards

⑨ TODAY	**⑩ TODAY**
What is coming up in the near future that you are looking forward to? Why? 	What will you do after school today? Describe the activities. 
Classbuilding Questions • © Kagan Publishing	*Classbuilding Questions* • © Kagan Publishing
⑪ TODAY	**⑫ TODAY**
On a scale of 1 to 10, how would you rate today? Explain your rating. 	If you could change one thing about today, what would you change? How would you change it? 
Classbuilding Questions • © Kagan Publishing	*Classbuilding Questions* • © Kagan Publishing

Classbuilding Questions
Kagan Publishing • (800) 933-2667 • www.KaganOnline.com

TODAY
Question Cards

13 TODAY

If you could re-live today, would you do it? Why or why not?

Classbuilding Questions • © Kagan Publishing

14 TODAY

What are all the important events that happened yesterday that you can remember? Describe them.

Classbuilding Questions • © Kagan Publishing

15 TODAY

Pick someone from your family and describe how your day today is different from their day.

Classbuilding Questions • © Kagan Publishing

16 TODAY

What decisions did you make today? Are you happy with your decisions? Why or why not?

Classbuilding Questions • © Kagan Publishing

TODAY
Question Cards

17 TODAY

Did you do anything today that will influence your future? Explain.

Classbuilding Questions • © Kagan Publishing

18 TODAY

What role did the weather play on your day? Explain. Describe other ways that weather affects your day.

Classbuilding Questions • © Kagan Publishing

19 TODAY

How do you feel today and why?

Classbuilding Questions • © Kagan Publishing

20 TODAY

What does this quote by Albert Einstein mean to you: "Learn from yesterday, live for today, hope for tomorrow"? Explain your answer.

Classbuilding Questions • © Kagan Publishing

Classbuilding Questions
Kagan Publishing • (800) 933-2667 • www.KaganOnline.com

TODAY
Journal Writing Question

If you could change one thing about today, what would you change? How would you change it?

_____

_____

_____

_____

_____

_____

_____

_____

_____

_____

_____

_____

_____

_____

_____

_____

_____

TODAY
Journal Writing Question

What are all the important events that happened yesterday that you can remember? Describe them.

Classbuilding Questions
Kagan Publishing • (800) 933-2667 • www.KaganOnline.com

card set
#20

TRAVEL

TRAVEL
Question Cards

TRAVEL

1 Where is the most interesting place you've ever been? Why did you find it so interesting?

Classbuilding Questions • © Kagan Publishing

TRAVEL

2 Where is the farthest place you've traveled to away from your home? Where did you go and what did you do?

Classbuilding Questions • © Kagan Publishing

TRAVEL

3 Would you rather travel the world for an entire year or stay at home? Explain.

Classbuilding Questions • © Kagan Publishing

TRAVEL

4 Do you prefer going to warm tropical places or cold snowy places? Why?

Classbuilding Questions • © Kagan Publishing

TRAVEL
Question Cards

5 TRAVEL

Are you more interested in visiting mountainous areas where you could hike, ski, and explore or beaches where you can relax, surf, and read? Explain.

Classbuilding Questions • © Kagan Publishing

6 TRAVEL

When you travel, would you rather venture out to learn about the people in the places, or would you rather just stay in the hotel and relax by the pool? Explain.

Classbuilding Questions • © Kagan Publishing

7 TRAVEL

What are some of the things you don't like about traveling? Describe them.

Classbuilding Questions • © Kagan Publishing

8 TRAVEL

Would you rather travel by air, by sea, or by land? Explain.

Classbuilding Questions • © Kagan Publishing

TRAVEL
Question Cards

TRAVEL

9

Would you rather explore castles in Germany, the pyramids of Egypt, or the ancient ruins in Mexico? Why?

Classbuilding Questions • © Kagan Publishing

TRAVEL

10

Would you rather go on a wild animal safari in Africa, scuba dive off the Great Barrier Reef in Australia, explore the tropical rain forest of Brazil, or tour the ancient ruins of Greece? Explain your choice.

Classbuilding Questions • © Kagan Publishing

TRAVEL

11

What would you consider the most beautiful place on earth? Why?

Classbuilding Questions • © Kagan Publishing

TRAVEL

12

How would you feel if you travel to a country where no one spoke your language? What would you do to communicate?

Classbuilding Questions • © Kagan Publishing

Classbuilding Questions
Kagan Publishing • (800) 933-2667 • www.KaganOnline.com

TRAVEL
Question Cards

TRAVEL

13 If you could pick just one person to travel the world with, who would you pick and why?

TRAVEL

14 Which continent would you rather explore: Africa, Antarctica, Asia, Australia, Europe, North America, or South America? Explain your choice.

TRAVEL

15 Do you think people around the world are more alike or more different? Explain.

TRAVEL

16 What is the best souvenir you ever got from your travels or from someone else's travels? Describe it and how you got it.

TRAVEL
Question Cards

TRAVEL ⑰

Do you prefer the hustle and bustle of a big city, or a slow and laid-back sleepy town? Explain your choice.

TRAVEL ⑱

What is your idea of a fun adventure: sky diving, zip lining, bungee jumping, white water rafting, or surfing? Explain your choice.

TRAVEL ⑲

Which of these sounds like a fun experience: riding a camel through the desert, swimming with sharks, riding a dolphin, or trekking through the jungle on an elephant? Explain.

TRAVEL ⑳

What are some things you would like to see around the world in your lifetime?

TRAVEL
Journal Writing Question

What would you consider the most beautiful place on earth? Why?

_____

_____

_____

_____

_____

_____

_____

_____

_____

_____

_____

_____

_____

_____

_____

_____

_____

_____

_____

_____

TRAVEL
Journal Writing Question

Do you think people around the world are more alike or more different? Explain.

NOTES

NOTES

Classbuilding Questions
Kagan Publishing • (800) 933-2667 • www.KaganOnline.com

NOTES

Classbuilding Questions
Kagan Publishing • (800) 933-2667 • www.KaganOnline.com

NOTES

Classbuilding Questions
Kagan Publishing • (800) 933-2667 • www.KaganOnline.com